Thank You For

Your continued

Support.

Praise for

upside-down selling

"I know Ian and have seen his work. He identifies problems, finds solutions and saves clients money. That formula is at the heart of his new book, Upside-Down Selling. This quick read will help you and your team find and "bring online" the problem solvers in your own organization...team members who can increase both the top line and bottom line results... not by selling, but by solving."

—Donald J. Hurzeler,
Former CEO Zurich Insurance
and author of *The Way Up*

"Ian's Issue/Impact/Importance (I3) has completely shifted our mindset. For every business development opportunity, we now assess if the client has conveyed I3 surrounding the requirement which ensures we focus on the right opportunities."

—Marissa Levin
CEO Information Experts and Successful Culture
INC 5000 in 2009, 2010, 2011
Author of *SCALE: Your Extraordinary Advisory Board"*

"If you don't have the opportunity to see Ian Altman live, this is the next best thing! His energy, enthusiasm, and most importantly, his real-world content comes to life in this simple, but powerful book. It not only informs, it involves the reader from start to finish."

—Robert L. Jolles
President, Jolles Associates, Inc. and
best selling author of *Customer Centered Selling*

"Let's just cut to the chase folks. If you're in sales and ready to stop wasting your time with fruitless "work", then you need to read this book. If you're looking to give your team a much greater vision of sales success, networking, and referrals-- you need to read this book. And finally, if you really just want to sell more stuff-- you need to read this book. Ian's language and message in Upside Down Selling is clear, concise, and exactly the shot in the arm you and your sales staff need right now."

—Marcus Sheridan, The Sales LionAuthor of
Inbound and Content Marketing Made Easy

"Upside-Down Selling genuinely reflects Ian's approach to business development. His focus on the process of opportunity development is important and valuable. But his ability to help each of us recognize and utilize the skills and traits we already possess to drive success and growth in our business is the true gem of his message. Reading and implementing the strategies in this book will be time well spent."

—Tim R. Hawkins, CPA
President, LT Business Dynamics

"Ian Altman has written a powerful, must-read book for anyone who wants a practical, comfortable, integrity-based approach to driving unparalleled growth in business. Designed to comfortably engage your whole team, this book is filled with specific actions for anyone who wants to secure dramatic and incredible success. He raises the bar for targeting and winning business without gimmicks. Ian helps you identify, evaluate, and convert opportunities into clients. From his signature material on "issue, impact, and importance" to his acronym D.E.C.I.D.E., this book is packed with accessible, memorable, results-based mindsets and steps for any business leader seeking outrageous growth for his company."

—Suzi Pomerantz, Executive Coach and Author of
Seal the Deal: The Essential Mindsets for Growing
Your Professional Services Business"

"Ian has written a simple to read, easy to adapt, and practical book that will help you and your team solve client problems. The powerful concept of focusing on delivering value by solving client problems, illustrated with easy to understand examples, and practical steps you can put to use immediately, will be invaluable to you if you're interested in growing your business. If you want to stand above and apart from your competitors, you must read this book and you'll be on your way to increasing your company's revenue!"

—Les Smolin
CEO Executive Leadership Forum &
Group Chairman, Vistage International, Inc.

AN ALTMAN

up
side
down
SELLING

AN INTEGRITY-BASED

SALES APPROACH

TO AVOID

BEING PREDICTABLE

ISBN-13: 978-0-9857333-0-8

50% of the proceeds of Amazon sales for this edition benefit The Network for Teaching Entrepreneurship (NFTE.com). You can learn more about NFTE at the end of the book.

1st Edition

Contact Information: info@UpsideDownSellingBook.com

This publication is designed to provide accurate and authoritative information in regard to the subject matter covered. It is sold with the understanding that the publisher is not engaged in rendering legal, accounting, or other professional services via the publication. Please do not operate heavy machinery while reading this publication either in print or electronically.

about

ian k. altman

Ian Altman is a speaker, author, and strategic advisor to CEOs and partners of businesses that sell products and services to businesses, government, and high-net-worth individuals. Ian works with hundreds of CEOs and firm partners each year to address their business development challenges with Upside-Down Selling

Ian is published in SmartCEO Magazine, is a weekly contributor to the Washington Business Journal's BizBeat, and entertains and educates readers via his popular blog at GrowMyRevenue.com.

Before forming Grow My Revenue, Ian spent two decades as founder and CEO of two companies, a consulting company and a software company. After successfully combining and then selling his companies, he served as managing director of the acquiring company. In that capacity, over the next three years he grew valuation ten-fold.

Ian helps businesses become outrageously successful targeting and winning business.

Please connect with Ian on Facebook or Twitter

 GrowMyRevenueFans

 @GrowMyRevenue

Look for Ian's forthcoming book in 2013.

dedication

This book is dedicated to my wonderful wife, Deborah, and our amazingly talented children who together provide inspiration, support, laughter, and a clear reminder of what matters each and every day.

acknowledgments

Much like creating a baby, it's tough to create a book alone. Several talented individuals provided tremendous input that helped to shape the content and style of this book.

Derek Coburn (Cadre)

Tom Cooper (BrightHill Group)

Steve Dorfman (Driven to Excel)

Jim Goldstein (Powerful Partnerships)

Babak Hafezi (Hafezi Capital)

Marissa Levin (Successful Culture)

Lowell Nerenberg (Coach Lowell)

Suzi Pomerantz (Innovative Leadership International)

Jeff Siegel (Jeff Siegel Creative)

Chris Yoko (Yoko Co)

what is upside-down selling?

Upside-Down Selling takes just about everything you know about the selling process and turns it on its ear – upside-down, if you will…

★ That means shifting the mindset from "pushing for sales" to **delivering value.**

★ That means getting away – far away! – from the traditional stereotypical perception of salespeople as plaid-jacket-wearing, lying weasels.

★ And that means achieving outrageous success by comfortably engaging your entire team to **grow revenue.**

★ With Upside-Down Selling, you'll quickly realize that your greatest growth potential is sitting right under your nose.

what lies below?

North Dakota has not exactly held an envied reputation, historically. Its greatest claim to fame was as the home of Mount Rushmore (which is actually in South Dakota). The movie, **Fargo**, could have been its reputational high point. But, most of the people in this all but forgotten territory did not realize that they had opportunity right under their feet: oil. Initial investigations, however, left people feeling it was impossible to realize the potential that awaited them just under the surface.

Experts threw up their hands and decided there was no way to reach the oil that lay below. Harold Hamm, president of Continental Resources, took the initiative to see if they could find a better way to extract value. They pioneered new drilling methods. Today, the Bakken Formation that spans Montana and North Dakota is one of the few places in the United States where there are more jobs than people. The Bakken Formation, by some estimates, is expected to produce more than one million barrels per day of domestic oil. With oil prices at about $100 per barrel, the value could exceed $35 billion a year. In the past, some might have suggested that the United States should have given North Dakota to Canada. Not anymore.

Is there value beneath the surface in your organization? What if you could access untapped resources within your business to drive strategic growth? Even with a dedicated sales and business development team, you are probably barely scratching the surface unless you discover how to engage your organization's non-sales professionals. These non-sales professionals are trusted advisors who are in regular contact with clients. Though they are experts at their craft, they are rarely comfortable engaging in business development activities. Explosive growth requires their help.

What could be the impact of a minor improvement in their ability to help grow revenue? From published research cited [1] in this book, we know that the most successful companies invest time in educating their non-sales teams on sales and business development approaches. But not any sales-type training will do. Effective training is not about persuasion and gimmicks. Rather, to have lasting impact, you need a way to develop and communicate a consistent process that each and every team member can follow to help expand opportunities within and beyond existing clients.

In Upside-Down Selling, you will discover how you can:

★ **Select team members who can uncover growth opportunities**

★ **Identify the process to position those team members for success**

★ **Define the steps to qualify opportunities and avoid wasted time**

★ **Enhance the value of your network with a disproportionately high share of quality referrals**

★ **Each chapter starts with a brief story. I then explain the lesson of the story, and conclude each chapter with "Upside-Down Selling in Action," a quick review which includes specific steps you can take to put the principles to work in your business. With a little effort, you can take one valuable step toward becoming outrageously successful at targeting and winning business.**

contents

finding hidden talent in your team

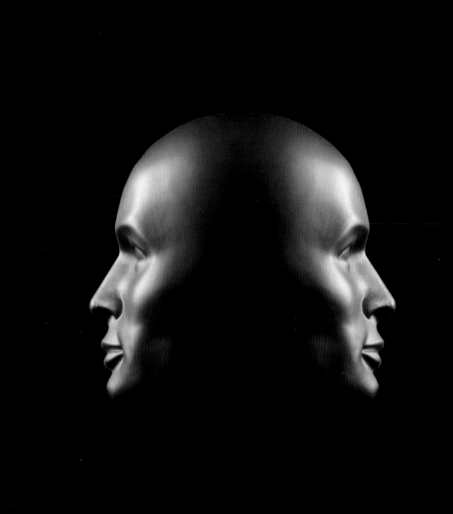

Wendy started a consulting company eight years ago. When times were good, they grew at a consistent pace. Recently, however, Wendy was trying to grow her business in a struggling economy. She had 90 professionals doing great work for 37 different clients. She had a business development team of four, including herself. Wendy knew that the firm had to grow in order to continue to create career opportunities for her talented team.

Wendy explained that she contemplated hiring a couple of new salespeople, but it would take time to get them up to speed. I asked, "Why don't we see if the other 80+ people in the company could help?" Wendy laughed out loud. "I've suggested that in the past," she said. "My team feels that being involved in sales undermines their role as trusted advisor to their clients. If they start pitching the clients, then their credibility goes out the window."

I nodded in agreement, and then asked, "What if your professionals felt comfortable that they could help grow the business while not only maintaining, but enhancing their position with the clients?" Wendy smiled, but showed some skepticism. Still, she arranged a meeting with three of her top people.

I started the conversation by asking, "What do salespeople do?" The answers were priceless:

- "Try to convince our clients they need things they don't need...."
- "Make promises that as a company we can't fulfill...." and my favorite:
- "Show up with a capabilities briefing and see if they can get the client to sign an agreement for more services while they are in a PowerPoint-induced coma."

The days of selling things your client does not need are over. I said to Wendy's group, "I don't blame you for not inviting salespeople to your meetings. If I felt that way, salespeople would not even have access to the building."

I then asked the consultants what they did, fundamentally, for their clients. One talked about his role in project management, another spoke about her role in technology, and another focused on training. When we got past the specifics of their jobs, there was a consensus: "We help our clients solve problems in a way they could not solve them on their own." With that revelation, I asked, "Would you feel uncomfortable being on the lookout for other problems you can solve for the client, provided that we put in place a business development process that is centered around solving problems, and not selling stuff?" They all nodded happily in agreement.

Fast forward one year, and Wendy's team has over 130 professionals deployed at 41 clients. The sales team has a new approach (and a new team member who replaced one who could not make the adjustment). The consultants and business development team work hand-in-hand to help their clients solve complex problems the clients could not solve themselves. They get more referrals both inside and outside of their existing accounts.

how can you produce the same results?

Many companies look at their "sales team" as their single source of revenue. But, what if you either a) don't have a formal sales team or b) realize that you have many customer-facing professionals who work every day with clients, but do not play an active, current role in growing revenue? Is it possible that those existing clients could benefit from more of your services? Let's face it: If you are a law/accounting/architectural firm, most of your so-called selling comes from professionals who have been tagged as rainmakers.

Fortunately, and contrary to popular belief, rainmaking skills can be taught well after birth. The challenge is that although you can learn every aspect of law, accounting, technology, and business in the various outstanding academic institutions, very few schools teach anything useful about how to grow your business. The shock comes when third-year associates quickly learn that, despite their amazing talent in their profession, advancement has almost everything to do with their ability to increase revenue.

How can you find valuable talent within your organization who could help to expand your opportunities?

Research supports the fact that the most effective people in sales are experts and consultants[2]. Though every person in the organization should be conscious of opportunities for revenue growth, there are some skills that you may want to seek or cultivate to increase the value of your non-sales staff in the sales and business development process.

"…the days of selling things your clients do not need are over"

As I said to Wendy's group, the days of selling things your clients do not need are over. Instead, you must focus on significant challenges your clients face where you might be able to offer a solution. Be on the lookout for the following characteristics in your non-sales staff.

Subject Matter Expertise: Clients are most likely to value individuals who have experience in their industry, have solved specific issues, or have valued credentials that might reduce risk for the client. Just saying that you have sharp people is not enough. You need to demonstrate tangible outcomes. Identify staff who have experience delivering results.

Active Listeners / Creative Thinkers: In selling situations, most professionals have learned the importance of questions. However, active listening is an equally important art that must be mastered. Active listening means being fully-engaged with the client and listening for the answers within the answers. You can tell when someone is "half listening," and so can your clients. Once you hear their needs, creativity can get you from concept to cash. Though every project needs people who can just do what they are told, the best contributors in selling situations have that creative spark to design solutions — but only when they have fully uncovered the impact behind the issues.

Project Management Skills: In order to reach an outcome on a sales opportunity, professionals need to manage a schedule, identify dependent tasks, track action items, and accept and assign responsibility. These are the same types of attributes found in effective project managers. Not every project manager can help in sales and business development, but the best closers understand the detail and "risk seeking" required to reach a timely decision with the client — and those skills are often found within good project managers.

Take an inventory of these skills in your team. Many (but not all) of these skills can be taught. Notice that I did not mention closing. If your team members have the skills above, closing is not about pressure. If you take the time to teach your team critical steps like listening, developing creative solutions, and taking responsibility, closing becomes an easy part of the process.

upside-down selling
in action

★ **Schedule a meeting within the next 30 days to describe how you plan to grow by helping clients solve more of their problems.**

★ **Identify three of your most curious individuals within 30 days after that meeting — the ones who are never satisfied with the superficial answer. That challenging mindset might be just what you need.**

★ **Invest in educating the same three individuals as part of a journey to understand the business development process in the next chapter.**

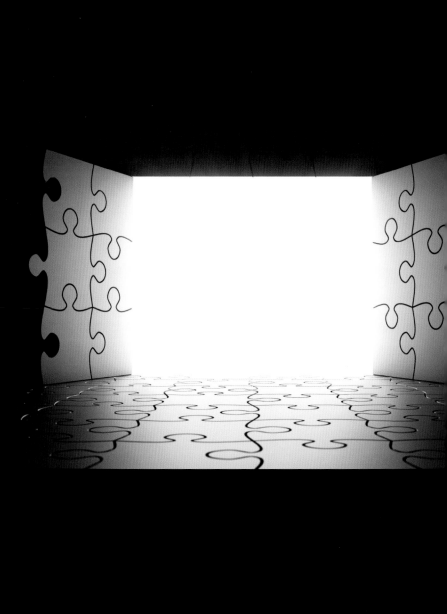

opportunity identification

Early in one of my businesses, I had a team of people working at a major pharmaceutical company. We were focused on a project to accelerate, review, and deliver new drug application (NDA) submissions to the U.S. Food and Drug Administration. You may already know that a new drug application can exceed one million pages per document. The NDA contains all of the material that the FDA uses to approve or deny a drug seeking to enter the market. The pharmaceutical industry generally attributes a $1 million savings to each day shaved from the process. Needless to say, we were involved in a mission-critical area of their business.

A few years down the road, we noticed the client was implementing a document imaging system. I thought, "Why didn't they ask us about it?" The client must have known that we had previously developed a document imaging product, right? But we were happy doing the work we were doing. We didn't think much more of it.

Over time, the company doing the document imaging started to expand the work they were doing. All of a sudden, they were playing a role in the NDA process. I commented to my on-site project lead, Tim, "I wish we had known about this imaging project before it started." Tim said, "They were talking about it for almost a year before it started. I don't know why they didn't ask us." At that moment, it all became clear.

The client had been having an open discussion with my team. Since my guys didn't mention anything, the client assumed we could not help them. Not only did we miss the opportunity for more business, but the other vendor was starting to encroach on our project. The imaging project was important for the client to pursue, and they went outside to find help. Too bad our team at the time did not know how to handle the situation.

● ● ●

The prospect can either say

a) "they are coming to pitch us on their services; or

b) "they are coming to talk to us about the XYZ problem to see if they can help"

● ● ●

how can you avoid making the same mistake?

Clients often wish their vendors offered additional services. As it turns out, over 85% of the time, just like the pharmaceutical company story, companies actually offer the very services clients hoped their vendors offered[3]. If the client doesn't realize that you offer the services they are looking for, they will likely find them elsewhere. And, there is a chance that the new vendor will also be able to perform the services your client already receives from you. Not only do you need to get to those opportunities for your growth, but you also need to understand that doing so may help you to retain your valuable clients.

So, what are some of the things you can do to identify additional opportunities within your existing client base?

If your business provides ongoing services, your primary point person is likely an associate, project manager, or principal. And, last time we checked, most of your associates don't have the most favorable impression of salespeople. By reputation, many professionals assume salespeople are trying to sell to people who don't need our help. That's why just asking your team to observe other professionals engaged in business development is not sufficient.

Top performing companies invest in educating their non-salespeople in the business development process[4]. But, what does that really mean?

Should you teach them how to be super-salespeople … wearing a cape and knocking down change orders in a single bound? Not hardly. But, by carefully demonstrating how they can help the client using a consultative process, those non-salespeople might develop confidence and comfort.

to start, you have to D-E-C-I-D-E:

DEPUTIZE RAVING FANS

There are opportunities every day to create a remarkable experience that turns otherwise satisfied clients into "raving fans" who will broadcast your wonderfulness to the world. There is a huge difference between happy customers and "net promoters[5]." Your raving fans become deputies for you and your business. There are few things you can do that are more compelling than having a raving fan tell a potential client how wonderful you are.

ESTABLISH A CONSULTATIVE METHOD

Companies want to buy from organizations that can help them solve their problems — the ones they already recognize and the ones they might not even realize yet. The best way to accomplish that is to take the time to learn what they need through a consultative process. If your team is going to meet with a senior executive at your client, how does the client describe the meeting to their peers? The prospect can either say a) "They are coming to pitch us on their services or" b) "They are coming to talk to us about the XYZ problem to see if they can help." Which version would your clients give? (Hint — we are looking for answer "b")

COMMUNICATE YOUR PROCESS

Knowing when to say yes or no is critical.

Ensure that each person in your organization understands your defined business development process, and the information you need to make informed decisions along the way. It's not enough to talk about it. Write it down and discuss how it is in the best interest of your organization and your clients. Your professionals are probably the same people who invest countless hours creating and submitting proposals for work that will never happen. The right process will reduce the amount of time people waste on fruitless pursuits.

IDENTIFY ROLES

Just like in a theatrical performance, each person plays a different role in the business development process. The casting agent is not expected to edit the film any more than your project manager is expected to take the deal to closure. Your goal for non-salespeople is to identify areas where your organization might be able to help the client. At that point, the non-salespeople might know that once they meet a certain threshold, they introduce other cast members who can take the next step.

DEFINE CRITERIA

Help your non-salespeople detect opportunities where you may be able to help your clients. There may be criteria for specific types of client problems and circumstances that your organization is especially well-suited to address. There may also be criteria for opportunities that you know you will not win. Knowing when to say yes or no is critical. Some opportunities may look nice, but may not be realistic or profitable for you to pursue.

ESTABLISH A HAND-OFF

Once your non-salespeople identify a potential opportunity, be sure to keep everyone informed. It is important to not damage the trust your team has established. Once someone in business development gets introduced, communication internally is critical. If it turns out that you cannot solve the issue for the client, it is just as critical to communicate that information as it would be to communicate the news that you landed new business. This is a learning experience, and transparent communication between team members will build trust and improve outcomes going forward.

Following these steps might help you earn more than your fair share of available business, improve communication among your team members, and may even get your formerly passive team members to be more active in growing your business. Use the acronym **D-E-C-I-D-E** to remember the steps.

upside-down selling in action

★ **Establish and communicate a plan with your team to educate your clients on areas where you can help them.**

★ **Set a goal of creating at least two raving fans in the next 60 days who will tell the world about your wonderfulness.**

★ **Schedule a specific date for an initial session to train your team on your consultative process.**

★ **Define a schedule to reinforce the training and make adjustments.**

★ **Agree on criteria for qualified opportunities.**

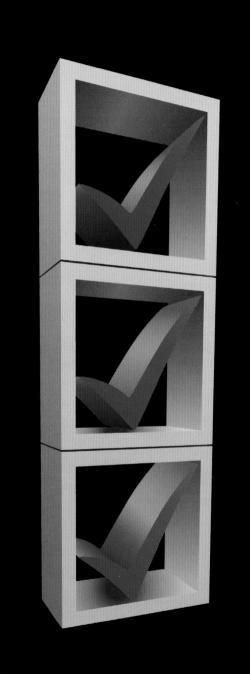

opportunity
qualification

Chris has an information technology company that maintains computer equipment and networks for his customers. They do this work on a fixed-fee basis, unlike most of his competition who charge everything by the hour. The challenge is that every one of their potential clients already has an existing solution to manage their technology. Some use internal resources, others already use an outside firm to manage their systems. In the past, Chris would ask potential clients, "Are you happy with how your systems are being managed and supported?" Regrettably, Chris was not seeing much success. Chris's message relied on the assumption that the client had already identified an issue to solve. Most of the people he contacted probably had little understanding of why they might feel that their IT staff or vendor was or was not doing a great job.

> • • •
>
> **If the client cannot convince you that the problem is worth solving, then why would you invest time on a solution?**
>
> • • •

We changed Chris's message to focus beyond the issue, and instead consider the impact of what his company did. Specifically, they would call a prospect in a professional services business and say, "Our clients tell us that they are sick of their staff not being able to perform billable work because their systems are not working. They also hate paying their outsource vendor to fix problems that it appeared the technology vendor itself originally created." The response was dramatic. Coupled with a good process for managing sales, Chris's company quickly grew their business larger than competitors that had been in existence five times longer.

"Your clients don't want *hours*, they want to solve a business challenge"

what can you do to achieve rapid growth like chris?

First — Remember to explain to your team members who serve as trusted advisors that their role is to identify opportunities where clients have a problem that your company might be able to solve. Trusted advisors should not be expected to "close" deals. Maintain focus on the client's needs. It is easy to rush to translate the client's problem into "head count" or "additional hours." Your clients don't want hours, they want to solve a business challenge. So, be sure to focus on their issue, not your billing. If you can help them identify the problem, the revenue will follow. Be patient. Think Upside-Down.

Second — Don't try to solve the problem on the fly. Rather, try to best understand the client's need or "issue." Jumping into the solution too early might halt the discussion and that diversion might prevent you from learning their true need.

There are other risks in jumping into the solution: The most common mistake is offering a solution that looks strikingly similar to something they already tried without success. Exercise patience and discipline to learn more about the client's problem, including what has and has not worked for them. If your approach is similar to one that already failed, you want to be able to explain why your approach is different than their previously failed attempt.

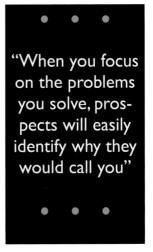

"When you focus on the problems you solve, prospects will easily identify why they would call you"

Third — Primitive sales and business development systems taught that qualification was all about three things: Need, Budget, and Authority. Although those factors are important, they tend to get you to focus on what you think you want to know to make a sale and not what your clients need to solve an issue or create new possibilities. If you focus on their needs, you maintain your role as trusted advisors instead of becoming someone trying to sell something they may not need.

in today's world, the three things that matter are issue, impact, and importance (i3):

Issue — What is the problem they are trying to solve?

Impact — How is their organization impacted by NOT solving the problem? For commercial clients, Impact tends to translate to dollars of cost savings or new revenue. In other cases, it might be that not solving the Issue could Impact the client's ability to meet their strategic objectives.

Importance — How important is it to the person you are working with to solve the Issue? Just because they have an Issue that appears to have Impact of $5 million per year doesn't make it a top priority. If they have bigger fish to fry, you may need to be sensitive to timing. If it is not on their top three list, it probably won't happen.

If the **Issue**, **Impact**, and **Importance** are sufficient, they'll find the money … and they'll be receptive to a discussion about solving that challenge for their organization. This might be the most Upside-Down of all of the concepts: If the client cannot convince you that the problem is worth solving, then why would you invest time on a solution?

upside-down selling in action

★ **Focus on client needs instead of your products and services.**

★ **Be patient. Uncover the details. Don't jump the gun.**

★ **Define specific target criteria that you are seeking. Be focused rather than broad.**

★ **Qualify based on I3: Issue, Impact, and Importance.**

quality
referrals

in three easy steps

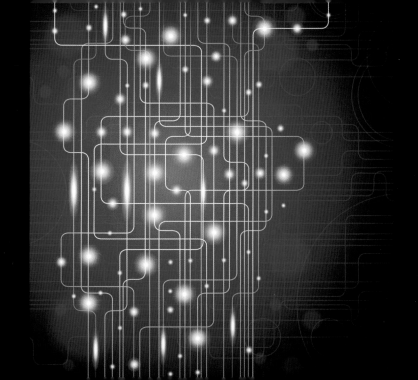

Brad has a health insurance agency. He was sharing some stories about major successes with some of their clients. In each story, he was able to articulate the tremendous work his team performed, the incredible value the client received as a result of their efforts, and the trusted advisor status the client had bestowed upon Brad and his team. Brad was creating remarkable results for his clients. For example, Brad's clients were not seeing their premiums rise, whereas others were seeing double digit increases.

I asked Brad how well he was meeting his growth objectives. Brad commented that despite these great accomplishments, they were spending most of their time cold-calling or responding to RFPs. What's more, they were getting to the RFPs too late in the game, and he was frustrated that his referral network was not delivering. He had some raving fans, but those fans were not translating to revenue growth.

how could a team with such incredible performance not get their fair share of referrals?

When you are doing great work for your clients, it is easy to focus on expanding into other opportunities within that same account. But, what about growing in other areas of their organization, or beyond their walls entirely? One of the keys to growing your business is getting good referrals. Even if you attend many events and have developed a huge network of contacts, like Brad, you may find that you are not getting your fair share of good referrals from your contacts. Here are three keys to getting your "better than fair" share of referrals.

FOCUS ON PROBLEMS (SYMPTOMS)

It's easy to tell people about the services you provide. Think Upside-Down: Instead, talk about the types of problems you solve. Your potential clients and those who would refer you to them know they have some problems, but they may not realize that your services provide the solution.

As an example, let's say you are experiencing unexplained leaks around the outside of your house. You may not realize that a roofing contractor would address downspouts, gutters, and flashing to fix that type of problem. But, you would certainly know that you have leaks around the house. So, if a roofer looking for referrals told his friends, "Please let me know if you know someone who needs a roofer," even if one of his friends knew you and heard of your problem, he might not think to refer them to you. Suppose, instead, the roofer said to his network, "We solve the problem of unexplained water entering our clients' homes, whether it is coming from the roof, the ground, or anywhere in between. Our clients also come to us to find solutions to their crazy utility bills by helping improve their home's efficiency." In that case, he would likely get a referral to help you with your leaks.

As another example, if you are an accountant, instead of just saying, "We are a full-service accounting firm," you might tell more of a story that illustrates your successes with other clients. One such story might sound like this: "The CEO of a new client was not confident in the financial data they were using to make business decisions. A bad decision could cost them hundreds of thousands of dollars. Within 90 days, we took responsibility, established a consistent process, and now their executives rest easy that they have clear, reliable information on which to base important decisions." When you focus on the problems you solve, prospects will easily identify why they would call you.

BE A SPECIALIST

I'm sure you have either referred someone or been referred to a physician, professional, or other vendor. When was the last time you heard someone refer to someone as "a great generalist"? Your natural inclination is to favor someone who is great at doing something specific. Carve your niche, and emphasize that expertise to your clients and referrers. Even if your organization has amazing breadth, recognize that you get rewarded for being specific. If you say that you do everything, people are not likely to believe you. Be clear and explicit about the things you do better than the average bear, and seek opportunities where you can differentiate yourself (with a straight face). If you can share stories of specific problems that you solved for real customers, it's easy for someone to make the connection to their situation. With specific examples, it's easy for them to say, "I know that they solved problem A for one of their clients."

Law firms and accounting firms often struggle with this notion of specialization. Instead of leading by saying, "We are a large regional law firm with x number of partners in all areas of law," try a more specific approach: "I help technology companies ensure that their inventions are protected and that others cannot interfere with their business (and then share a real-world story). As a large regional firm, I have partners right down the hall skilled in solving a wide array of legal and business challenges. If you refer someone we'll always be able to identify the best people to help." In this case, being specific helps sharpen your focus and en-sure that the referrer knows your specialty. They'll assume the other partners each have their own focus, too.

BE SMART

I often hear people say, "If you know someone who needs my service, please let me know." How often do you think that person gets referrals? They have two chances: slim and none. SMART is an acronym that stands for Specif-ic, Measurable, Attainable, Relevant, and Timely. (The "R" can also stand for "realistic," but, I confuse that with "At-tainable.") So, you might try something like "Do you think you could identify two clients in the next 30 days who are experiencing the problem we discussed, and make an introduction?" In this example, we are specific with a mea-surable, attainable, and relevant (and realistic) goal tied to a specific timeframe. You'd be amazed at the dramatic change this can have.

So, if you want to earn your "better than fair share" of refer-rals, remember to 1) Focus on Problems, 2) Be Specific, and 3) Be SMART. And don't feel like you have to make the identical request to each potential referrer. Based on their sphere of influence, you might have different requests for each person in your network. And, if you happen to have a breadth of problems you solve, feel free to "specialize" in areas that fit that member of your network.

upside-down selling
in action

★ **Define a list of problems you solve (not features and benefits). Think in terms of the complaints a decision maker at your client might say to their colleague.**

★ **Establish an area of focus where your past experience demonstrates credibility in a specific domain.**

★ **Create a referral script that is SMART, and practice it with a colleague until it flows naturally.**

★ **Document a plan for contacting three referral sources per week and track the results.**

a case study in
upside down selling™

Now that you've read **Upside-Down Selling**, this bonus chapter will help you discover how a company, hopefully not unlike your company, implemented **Upside-Down Selling** in their business.

Excella Consulting has their headquarters in the Commonwealth or Virginia, just across the river from Washington, DC. Excella is an information technology consulting company who boasts a top-tier client base that strikes an even balance between commercial and federal government clients. Excella's culture sets it apart from the competition. Their culture stands as a foundation to attract and retain top talent in the industry. The company is run by five partners, and a capable management team. When they wanted to grow, the partners concluded that they needed an integrity-based approach that would in no way put their trusted advisor role at risk. Excellians (their term for Excella team members) have worked hard to earn their positions of trust.

The leadership team had seen too many examples of other organizations who had tried to grow by adding traditional salespeople. In those organizations, the culture would rapidly erode, along with the company's trust, reputation, talent, and eventually their clients and revenue. Excella had grown to over one hundred Excellians without an individual in a traditional sales or business development role. Maintaining the status quo, the company was on track to grow eleven percent. But, top-performing companies like Excella rarely follow the status quo.

Growth for Excella is not about ego. Excella's leadership knows that creating opportunities for their team members to grow and assume additional responsibilities provides a solid foundation for retention and recruitment of the stellar talent in their stable. Indeed, Excella wanted to grow, but needed to identify a method to engage their entire team of Excellians to further build upon their culture.

> ●   ●   ●
>
> Our people generally don't like the idea of selling, but they love solving problems. Upside-Down Selling helped us make that mindset shift away from selling and into solving problems. It unlocked a ton of potential in our people and the firm overall.
>
> Jeff Gallimore
> Co-Founder, Excella
>
> ●   ●   ●

I had the honor of working closely with Excella's leadership to implement ***Upside-Down Selling*** in their organization. We worked together, meeting several times per month to implement the ***Upside-Down Selling*** steps. They were kind enough to share their experience, their results, and most importantly their lessons learned.

STEP ONE - PROBLEMS WE SOLVE

Like many organizations, Excella delivered exceptional capabilities and results. From a marketing perspective, however, their business focus was communicated from their own perspective rather than their client's perspective. Excella had built centers of excellence around Agile development, Microsoft's platform, Java, business analysis, and the federal government.

If someone asked about their business, they would say "Excella is an IT consulting company helping clients develop and execute strategies to use technology. We have deep expertise in Java and .NET development, and a particular focus on Agile methodologies." For starters, it sounded quite a bit like everyone else. But, that's not all.

The challenge is that potential clients often would not know why they needed those services. The people who did understand those services tended to be technologists rather than the business or operations people directly impacted. The technical people viewed those capabilities as commodities, or thought they could figure it out on their own. In contrast, the line of business leaders at their client organizations may not understand the underlying technology, but they had a complete understanding of the problems and frustrations they faced. Excella needed to shift its focus away from WHAT Excella did, and instead focus on WHY the clients needed them. In essence, what problems could they solve?

A toddler would be an excellent facilitator of this exercise. Have you ever been interrogated by a toddler who keeps asking "why" to every answer you give? I follow a similar model. The goal is to draw consensus from the leadership about where the organization has differentiation in the market, and what customers would say about their greatest value. Excella's partners collaborated to define key areas where they help clients solve issues better than the average bear. What started as a list of more than twenty eventually evolved into a laser-sharp description: "Our clients hire us when their software does not work, they can't make sense of their data, or their often-late and over-budget projects don't solve the problems they were supposed to address. "This concise message hits the core of where Excella's clients see them adding the most value.

STEP TWO - FIND HIDDEN TALENT

Excellians possess strong subject matter expertise, are active listeners and creative thinkers, and excel at project management tasks. Excella's challenge was not to identify three qualified individuals, but how many people could they enable at once. Excella maintains an internal, professional development program called Excella U. They conduct regular training programs for their team on a wide range of topics. Historically, those topics included technical or project management areas. Most courses are taught by Excella's subject matter experts or individuals leading a particular center of excellence.

STEP THREE - DEPUTIZE THE TROOPS

Excella embarked on a three-stage approach to engage their untapped growth engine found within their organization. First, they communicated the problems they solve to the management team. The partners made it clear that if the approach was not integrity-based, or if the managers did not feel comfortable, then they would have to shift gears. Everyone was on board.

Next, Excella communicated to their team that Excella U would add a class on business development. The class attendance was voluntary, and was scheduled in the evening. Dinner was provided. The class was sold out. Attendees discovered how to identify areas where Excella helps its clients. Excella had no interest in selling things clients did not need. Rather, their mission was to find areas where their clients were struggling with technology-related business challenges where Excella's assistance would be welcomed. Each attendee learned how they could help, and specifically what their role would be in the process. They also learned how to transition the opportunity to a member of Excella's leadership.

STEP FOUR - GO DEEP

Excella U added an additional class for the **Upside-Down Selling** Immersion. Since it was a full-day program, it had to be offered on a holiday. The class was optional. As in the previous class, the course was full with a waiting list. Attendees learned the entire end-to-end consultative process for growing business. They engaged in role playing. They discovered how to comfortably engage clients in discussions about other challenges they face, and even how to get referrals within and beyond the current client organization.

STEP FIVE - GET HANDS-ON

Excella leadership held individual meetings with each project manager to review their accounts, evaluate potential areas where the client might need additional support, and planned an approach to determine how Excella could help.

DELIVER RESULTS

Excella was growing successfully at 11% per year. In the first six months after implementing the program, the company expanded within and beyond existing clients to provide more value. This increase in demand has driven the need to add more than forty new Excellians to the company. Growth in the first full year is on track to more than double its previous rate. During the same time, Excella has earned an average client satisfaction grade of 3.9 out of 4.0. So, not only is business growing, but Excella's clients remain quite satisfied with their level of service. More remarkably, Excella continues to grow and thrive while many in their field have seen their business shrink. They have maintained their gross margin while increasing revenue.

LESSONS LEARNED

Today, Excella's greatest challenge is recruiting top talent to keep pace with the demands for its services and expertise. Because they so greatly value their culture and high performance, Excella often interviews many candidates before making a single offer. They know that one bad apple can spoil the bunch. But, as their profile continues to rise, extraordinary professionals seek them out to join an elite team in an organization that values its employees and continues to thrive where others may struggle.

SUMMARY

Excella is an extraordinary company. They resisted the temptation to cast a wide net to chase opportunities, and instead narrowed their focus to where they create the most value for their clients. They ignored suggestions that they needed to hire a bunch of salespeople responsible for peddling their services, and instead invested in their team and entrusted them with the tools and training to expand how they were helping their clients. They turned the conventional approach on its ear to reinforce their culture and create an even stronger bond with their clients.

It required dedication, discipline, and an outstanding team. But, perhaps reading about their results is enough to make you believe you could become outrageously successful targeting and winning business in your organization.

WHAT'S NEXT?

Stay tuned for future Upside-Down Selling case studies about other extraordinary organizations.

MIND MAP FOR UPSIDE DOWN SELLING

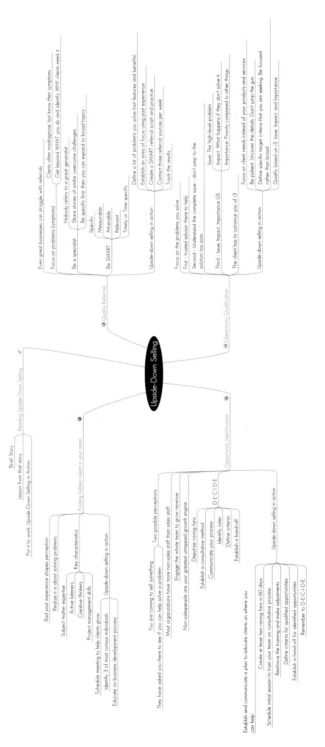

Upside-Down Selling

- Brief Story
  - Lesson from that story
  - Put it to work Upside-Down Selling in Action
- Reading Upside-Down Selling

Quality Referrals
- Even great businesses can struggle with referrals
- Focus on problems (symptoms)
  - Clients often misdiagnose but know their symptoms
  - Get beyond WHAT you do and identify WHY clients need it
- Be a specialist
  - Nobody refers to a great generalist
  - Share stories of similar overcome challenges
  - Be specific first, then you can expand to broad topics
- Be SMART
  - Specific
  - Measurable
  - Attainable
  - Relevant
  - Timely or Time specific
- Upside-down selling in action
  - Define a list of problems you solve (not features and benefits)
  - Establish an area of focus using past experience
  - Create a SMART referral script and practice
  - Contact three referral sources per week
  - Track the results

Opportunity Qualification
- Focus on the problems you solve
  - First - trusted advisor there to help
  - Second - Understand the complete issue - don't jump to the solution too soon
  - Third - Issue-Impact-Importance (i3)
    - Issue: The high-level problem
    - Impact: What happens if they don't solve it
    - Importance: Priority compared to other things
- The client has to convince you of i3
- Upside-down selling in action
  - Focus on client needs instead of your products and services
  - Be patient. Uncover the details. Don't jump the gun.
  - Define specific target criteria that you are seeking. Be focused rather than broad
  - Qualify based on i3. Issue, Impact and Importance

Opportunity Identification
- Bad past experience shapes perception
- Realize it is about solving problems
- Subject matter expertise
  - Active listeners
  - Creative thinkers
    - Key characteristics
  - Project management skills
- Schedule meeting to help clients grow
- Identify 3 of most curious individuals
  - Upside-down selling in action
- Educate on business development process
- You are coming to sell something
  - Two possible perceptions
- They have asked you there to see if you can help solve a problem
- Most organizations have more non-sales staff than sales staff
- Engage the whole team to grow revenue
- Non-salespeople are your greatest untapped growth engine
  - Deputize roving fans
  - Establish a consultative method
  - Communicate your process
    - D-E-C-I-D-E
      - Identify roles
      - Define criteria
      - Establish a hand-off
- Establish and communicate a plan to educate clients on where you can help
  - Upside-down selling in action
- Create at least two raving fans in 60 days
- Schedule initial session to train your team on consultative process
  - Reinforce the training and make adjustments
  - Define criteria for qualified opportunities
  - Establish a hand-off for identified opportunities
  - Remember to D-E-C-I-D-E

conclusion
and next steps

Growing revenue does not happen accidentally. It is essential to have everyone in the organization focused on expanding opportunities. If done poorly, your team can feel like they are violating their role as trusted advisor. If, instead, you focus on helping your clients solve more of their problems, then your team will be comfortable expanding business opportunities while strengthening their trusted advisor position.

Remember to follow these simple steps to get you on the right path toward Upside-Down Selling:

★ Look for the right talent on your team who might be able to identify new opportunities.

★ Define a consistent, repeatable process for defining good and bad opportunities. Remember to D-E-C-I-D-E.

★ Identify Issue, Impact, and Importance (I3) to sharpen focus

★ Be SMART to earn your large number of referrals

Follow these simple steps, and you might be surprised when your team masters Upside-Down Selling and helps you become outrageously successful targeting and winning business.

about

NFTE

Too many young people today drop out of school and struggle to break the cycle of poverty. Since 1987, the Network for Teaching Entrepreneurship (NFTE) has been inspiring young people to pursue educational opportunities, start their own businesses, and succeed in life. By providing entrepreneurship education programs relevant to the real world, **NFTE** empowers students to own their educations in and out of the classroom and to find their own path to success.

NFTE is the only global nonprofit organization solely focused on bringing entrepreneurship education to low-income youth. To date, NFTE programs have reached more than 350,000 young people. Currently, programs are active in 9 countries and 21 of the United States and NFTE impacts the lives of nearly 50,000 young people annually.

notes

1 Lee W. Frederiksen and Aaron E. Taylor, *Spiraling Up* (Reston, VA: Hinge, 2010), p. 26

2 Lynette J. Ryals and Iain Andrew Davies, *"Do You Really Know Who Your Best Salespeople Are?"* Harvard Business Review, 88:12 (December 2010).

3 Frederiksen and Taylor, Spiraling Up, p. 63

4 Ibid, p. 26

5 Jeremy Epstein, *"What Is Community Driven Marketing?"* Never Stop Marketing, August 24, 2009, http://jer979.com/are-your-customers-your-best-marketers/ accessed December 19, 2011.

You made it!
Next time,
try reading the book
upside
down

Please visit

UpsideDownSellingBook.com

for bonus content

on

Upside-Down Selling